"In *Lily, the Lemur and the Lamb King: The Me Tree and Other Adventures*, Bob Hartman offers whimsical stories featuring endearing characters whose escapades sneak past our defenses, capture our imagination, and lead us to delight in the Lord. With delicious surprise, I realized I was worshiping as I was reading. In a sense, these engaging stories grab children (and adults) by the hand, and say with excitement, 'Come with me, and I'll show you something wonderful!' I highly commend this lighthearted yet gloriously rich collection of stories to you and your family. You'll love it!"

CAROLINE SAUNDERS

Author, *The Story of Home* and *Kids in the Bible*

"Another quirky storybook from Bob, with the bouncy rhythm of the text that makes for great storytelling. This unusual take on the kingdom of God is full of fun but with moments of poignancy and plenty of space left for questioning imaginations."

LUCY MOORE

Head, Growing Faith Foundation

"Bob Hartman has done it again. The adventures of Lily, the Lemur and the Lamb King will delight both children and parents in their creative reimagining of stories from the Gospels. Bob is a great storyteller, but the beauty of this book is that it will introduce children to the greatest Storyteller of them all—Jesus."

JUSTIN BRIERLEY

Author, Speaker and Broadcaster

"Another fantastic Bob Hartman book! *Lily, the Lemur and the Lamb King* is a storybook full of joy. It's cleverly knitted together with kingdom principles and biblical themes, along with a healthy dose of comedy and playfulness. This is the perfect way to share the gospel and to start conversations about Jesus. Highly recommended!"

JOANNA ADEYINKA-BURFORD
TV Presenter and Author

"This book is a bit like Narnia. I liked all the characters, especially the big rabbit. It encouraged my faith in Jesus, the Lamb King."

ZANNA, aged 10

"I liked reading this book—I read it all in one day! I highly recommend it for readers big and small."

GABRIEL, aged 8

"This is a good story. The animals all have lots of adventures together, and I like having adventures too. Sometimes it was a bit sad, but all the different animals are good friends and they do good things together which makes them feel better again."

SOLOMON, aged 6

"I really enjoyed this book. I liked how it had lots of talking animals. My favourite was the really small elephant."

LIBBY, aged 8

WRITTEN BY: **BOB HARTMAN**

ILLUSTRATED BY: **KEILA ELM**

LILY, THE LEMUR AND THE LAMB KING

THE ME TREE & OTHER ADVENTURES

Lily, the Lemur and the Lamb King:
The Me Tree & Other Adventures
© Bob Hartman, 2025.

Published by:
The Good Book Company

thegoodbook.com | thegoodbook.co.uk
thegoodbook.com.au | thegoodbook.co.nz | thegoodbook.co.in

All Scripture References are taken from the Holy Bible, New International Version, NIV. Copyright © 1973, 1978, 1984, 2011 Biblica, Inc.™ Used by permission. All rights reserved.

All rights reserved. Except as may be permitted by the Copyright Act, no part of this publication may be reproduced in any form or by any means without prior permission from the publisher.

Bob Hartman has asserted his right under the Copyright, Designs and Patents Act 1988 to be identified as author of this work.

Keila Elm has asserted her right under the Copyright, Designs and Patents Act 1988 to be identified as illustrator of this work.

Illustrations by Keila Elm | Design and Art Direction by André Parker

ISBN: 9781802541359 | JOB-007974 | Printed in India

CONTENTS

1. The Lamb King	9
2. Tomorrow and Today	21
3. The Me Tree	29
4. The Ice-Cream Van	37
5. Upside Down	47
6. The Apple Argument	57
7. Nan's Handbag	65
8. Tigers and Tables	75
9. The Seesaw	85
10. The Hermit	95
11. Not That Kind of King	105
12. For Ever	113

The stories you're about to read are inspired by another, bigger story.

You might want to just read them and enjoy them as they are.

But you can also find out what inspired each story at the back of the book, starting on page 125.

1. THE LAMB KING

The morning was so beautiful, it was all Lily could do to keep from leaping.

She breathed in the fresh spring air. She smiled at the blossoming apple tree. Then she turned to her friend the Lemur, who was walking along the street beside her.

"What do you want to do today?" Lily asked.

"Dunno," the Lemur replied, looking down at the pavement and stepping gingerly over a banana peel. "Something interesting. But also something *safe*."

And that was when a Lamb skipped up and joined them.

Lily was surprised. "Haven't seen you before," she said. "But I like your pointy hat."

"It's a crown," chuckled the Lamb. "I'm the Lamb King!"

"Hmmm," said the Lemur. "You don't look much like a king."

"I get that a lot," the Lamb King smiled. And then he looked at Lily. Quite intently.

"Ninety-nine thousand and thirty-seven," he said.

"Ninety-nine thousand what?" asked Lily.

"Hairs on your head," said the Lamb King. "Just practising."

Then he reached out his arms—as down from the sky dropped a sparrow!

"Good catch!" cried the Lemur.

"Thanks," grinned the Lamb King.

But Lily gasped.

"Is it dead?" she said.

"It is, poor thing," the Lamb King replied. "But not for long."

He breathed on the sparrow, and up it fluttered and flew away.

"That's amazing!" said Lily. "How did you do that?"

"All I can say," grinned the Lamb King, "is that breathing is very important. Breathing. And playing."

And just as he said it, a gate, with a sign that said "Playground", appeared out of nowhere before them.

"Follow me," said the Lamb King, opening it.

But when Lily, the Lemur and the Lamb King stepped through the gate, there was nothing. Nothing at all. Everything was dark.

The Lamb King didn't seem worried. "Playtime!" he said. "Where do we start?"

"With some light, maybe?" suggested the Lemur nervously. "So we can see where we are going. There may be banana peels."

"Good idea!" replied the Lamb King. Then he drew in a big breath. "As I said, breathing is very important. And words. You can't do one without the other."

Then he shouted, "LIGHT!"... and everything went bright.

Lily rubbed her eyes. But the Lamb King was already moving on.

THE LAMB KING

"What next?" he asked. "How about some... SKY!"

And as soon as he'd said it, there it was. Bluey bright and cloudy white.

"What about WATER?" the Lamb King said next. And in a flash, they were floating in a sea. Lily and the Lamb King, with the Lemur perched on the Lamb King's head.

"I think I like land better," said the Lemur.

"Then land it is!" chuckled the Lamb King. "On the count of three, let's all leap up. One... two... three... And LAND!"

LILY, THE LEMUR AND THE LAMB KING

And there was earth, hard beneath their feet. Mountains and hills rose around them. And the water pooled into rivers and lakes and seas... and pools!

"Could we have some plants?" asked Lily.

"My thoughts exactly!" replied the Lamb King. "What kind?"

"Trees. Grass. Flowers," Lily listed.

The Lamb King looked high into the sky and cried, "TREEEEEES!"

The Lamb King looked down at the ground and grunted, "GRASS."

Then the Lamb King shut his eyes and leaned

back his head and, spinning round and round, whispered, "FLOWERS."

Lily jumped out of the way as a tree rose from the on which she stood, then she chased the carpet of grass as it spread along the ground. And when a garden of flowers followed, she called out the name of every one she knew. Including the lilies, of course!

Then the Lamb King took his new friends' hands and marched them to a hole in the ground.

"Where are we going?" Lily asked.

"To the MOOOON!" he laughed, and he pulled them into the hole before they could stop him.

They fell for what felt like for ever.

"I think I said something about *safe!*" the Lemur shouted.

But when they popped out of the other side of the hole, they found themselves in a huge, rocky crater.

"Are we on the moon?" gasped Lily as they climbed up the sides.

"Yes! And there's the sun!" The Lamb King pointed. "And just look at all those stars!" He tugged at the Lemur's fur. "Your eyes are big as saucers. Maybe even flying saucers!"

"It's just the way I'm made," said the Lemur.

Then they all held hands again, leaped back into the crater... and landed on the back of a...

"WHALE!" shouted the Lamb King. "And, look! Dolphins and sharks and tuna and trout."

"It's like a race!" Lily cried. "But where are we going?"

"There!" the Lamb King pointed. It was just a blur, at first, like an enormous cloud. But when he shouted, "BIRDS!", feathers and wings and beaks burst forth and flew straight for them.

Then down reached two talons and an enormous eagle lifted them into the sky.

"Yikes!" cried the Lemur. "Definitely not safe!"

"Yippeee!" shouted Lily. "I don't care!"

"That's the spirit!" the Lamb King shouted in reply.

When the eagle set them down on a grassy field, the Lamb King simply said, "ANIMALS."

And there they were, all in a line, to welcome Lily, the Lemur and the Lamb King.

"It's perfectly safe," said the Lamb King to the Lemur. "Be as friendly as you like."

"I'll stick to the plant eaters," said the Lemur. "If it's all the same to you."

But Lily patted a panther and played with a polar bear and tickled a timber wolf under its chin.

And when they came at last to the giraffe, the Lamb King led Lily and the Lemur dancing beneath its legs.

"Now it's time for my favourite word," he grinned. And what he said was, "PEOPLE".

Just like that, Lily, the Lemur and the Lamb King were back in the playground. And sure enough, people were everywhere—swinging and sliding, playing and picnicking, old and young, everyone!

"Can we do it again?" asked Lily.

"Another day, maybe," yawned the Lamb King. "I think I need a rest."

"Me too," agreed the Lemur. "This day was, quite

possibly, a little too interesting."

Then the Lamb King stared at a bald man sitting on a bench. Stared quite intently.

"Forty-seven." He chuckled. "Just practising!"

2. TOMORROW AND TODAY

"Another spring day!" said the Lamb King.

"Perfect!" Lily agreed, skipping along the playground path. "Sunny sun! Bluey sky! And no clouds at all!"

"But there *is* a cloud out there," said the Lemur, looking off into the distance. "And it's a dark one. You know how it is with spring. Sun one minute. Showers the next. I bet there's a storm coming."

"We'll deal with that tomorrow," the Lamb King replied. "No point worrying about it today."

"But we have to get ready!" worried the Lemur. "Find some shelter. A tree. A cave. A very large umbrella. My fur goes really frizzy when it gets wet!"

Lily wasn't listening. "Ooh, look," she said, pointing at the ground. "Look at those pretty daffodils."

"Yes. Lovely," said the Lemur reluctantly. Then he pointed, too. To where the sky met the ground. "Cloud! Dark cloud!"

"It sounds like you worry a lot, Lemur," said the Lamb King.

"Only because there is lots to worry about," the Lemur replied.

"Like what?" asked the Lamb King.

"What to eat, for a start," said the Lemur. "A wild animal like me has to spend an enormous part of each day searching through the jungle for the food he needs to survive. Dinner doesn't grow on trees, you know."

"I think you'll find that it does," said the Lamb King.

"And, besides," added Lily, "my nan packed a lunch for us. Look!"

She held out her lunch bag and the Lemur jammed his head right in.

"Hmmm," he noted. "Cookies. Cakes. Crisps. And do my big round eyes deceive me, or is that a mango?"

"Nan knows what you like," said Lily. "See, you didn't have to worry."

"But what about predators?" cried the Lemur. "There is a jungle full of toothy beasts—tigers, lions, wolves and the like—just itching to turn a little lemur like me into a snack, a sandwich or a stew."

"But there are no predators here," said Lily, looking round.

"Or maybe just none that you can see," the Lemur replied. "They are a sneaky lot, which is why, as my Uncle Lucky used to say, *a lemur who doesn't want to be dead is a lemur who looks ahead.*"

"Was he lucky, then?" asked the Lamb King.

"Let's just say that he passed away peacefully, not in some beastie's belly, but quietly, at home, a half-eaten hunk of mango dangling from his mouth. Every lemur's dream. As for luck, I would argue that he made his own luck, looking round every corner, carefully, just as I do."

"I have an idea," suggested the Lamb King with a

grin. "Why don't we keep on walking? Lily can look at what lies right around us. And, Lemur, you can look at what's up ahead and far away."

"Sounds good to me," Lily smiled. "Ooh, there's another bunch of daffodils!"

"Sounds good to me, too," said the Lemur. "Somebody has to do the sensible thing."

So off they walked, through the playground. Lily, the Lemur and the Lamb King.

"Hello, Mrs Red Breast," said Lily to a robin who had hopped right up to her.

"Very brave," said the Lamb King. "She must really be used to people."

"Not as brave as we're going to need to be," said the Lemur, ignoring the little bird

altogether, "when that big storm hits."

The robin cocked her head to one side and back again, then chirruped.

"I think she's trying to say something," Lily whispered.

"It's been a while since I talked to a robin," replied the Lamb King, "but I think she's saying that the Lemur shouldn't be so worried, because there is someone who knows what we need. And it's not just Lily's Nan."

"I heard that!" said the Lemur, his eyes still fixed on the horizon. "I bet that robin would sing a different tune if she knew there was a hawk out there."

"Is there?" asked Lily, worried.

"Well, no," the Lemur replied. "But there might be."

"There might be anything!" said the Lamb King. "But right here, right now, there is nothing but beauty surrounding us!"

"Like the cherry blossoms on that tree!" cried Lily. "Or that red squirrel. Or the little deer popping its head round that bush. And, Lemur, you're missing it all!"

"Yes, yes, yes," sighed the Lemur. "But by keeping my eye on that dark cloud, I'm making sure that we will all be safe!"

And then he said nothing else. Nothing else at all.

But the Lamb King did.

"Watch out!" he cried.

It was no use, though, as the Lemur fell into a pond that lay right in front of him. Splash!

The Lamb King reached down and helped out his spittering, sputtering friend.

"That's the other difficulty with worrying about the future," said the Lamb King. "You not only miss today's beauty. You may well miss today's problems, too."

The Lemur sighed. "Yes. Like what to do about all this frizzy fur!"

3. THE ME TREE

Lily and the Lemur looked up at a tree. A tree that stood just outside of the playground.

"Shall we climb it?" suggested Lily. "I love climbing!"

"I prefer dangling," replied the Lemur. "And eating, if I'm honest."

"I'm rubbish at climbing," said the Lamb King, his back planted against the trunk. "Hooves. Not really made for clinging on. So, what's your favourite tree?"

"Any tree with lots of forked branches," answered Lily.

"Any tree with lots of fruit," said the Lemur.

"How about you?"

The Lamb King rubbed his chin, thinking. "Any tree that has room for birds!" he said at last. "Lots and lots of birds."

Lily looked around.

"Can't see any of those," she said.

"Not yet," the Lamb King chuckled. "But they'll be here soon enough. You'll see."

And that was when the Lemur pointed at the tree and shouted, "Nuts! Look! It's not fruit. But it's food. And that's good enough for me."

Up the trunk he clambered. Along a branch he skipped. Then he grabbed an overhanging nut and popped it into his mouth.

"I wouldn't do that," said the Lamb King.

"Why not?" asked Lily.

"Yes, the shell. I know," the Lemur mumbled, his mouth full. "I have very strong teeth."

"It's not that," the Lamb King replied. "It's because there is somebody in there."

THE ME TREE

"What?" cried the Lemur, spitting the nut into his hand.

"Open it," said the Lamb King. "Have a look."

The Lemur pulled apart the shell. And, sure enough, there was a tiny man inside! He wore a tiny suit. He sported a tiny tie. And when he spotted the Lemur, he crossed his tiny arms in annoyance. Then the tiny man turned his back.

"What's he doing in there?" asked the Lemur

curiously, climbing down so that Lily could look at the little man, too.

"This is a Me Tree," said the Lamb King.

"A Me Tree?" asked Lily.

"Some people think only about themselves," explained the Lamb King. "They're selfish and their whole life is dedicated to putting themselves first and getting what they want."

"So is that what's going on with this little guy?" asked the Lemur.

"Possibly," the Lamb King replied. "Selfishness is not the only reason people end up in a Me Tree. Sometimes it's because they have been hurt. And they don't trust anybody anymore. Whatever the reason, what they don't realise is that this makes their lives smaller and smaller until…"

"Until they're all alone?" said Lily.

"Yes," sighed the Lamb King. "With a shell around them, made hard by their selfishness or by their sorrow."

THE ME TREE

"That's sad," Lily said.

"It is," agreed the Lamb King, taking the shell from the Lemur and gently closing it back up again. "Particularly when, like this little man, they can't even see it. But there is a different kind of tree. The kind I meant to show you. Follow me."

The Lamb King opened the gate to the playground and in they all went. Two families had just finished their picnic lunch. As they walked away, chatting, the Lamb King led Lily and the Lemur to the spot the family had left behind.

"Still can't see that tree," said Lily.

"All we need is a seed," the Lamb King replied. "And, look, there's one here on the ground."

"Erm, that's a sesame seed," said the Lemur. "On a bit of burger bun."

"Which makes it perfect!" cried the Lamb King. "You see, one of those families was new in town. And the other family invited them to join their picnic. To welcome them. To get to know them."

"And you know this, how?" asked the Lemur.

The Lamb King smiled. "I have very good hearing."

Then he planted the seed—and immediately, it began to grow.

Up and up and up it shot, its branches spreading wider as it went, like arms reaching out to the sky. And when it had finished growing, when it was big and bushy and broad, that was when the birds came. Flocks of them, settling into those branches, and calling out with a great cawing chorus.

"Cockerels and peacocks!" shouted Lily, pointing. "Sparrows and swallows! Blackbirds and mockingbirds and robins!"

"Every kind of bird!" the Lamb King grinned.

"And, strangely, a flying squirrel," noted the Lemur.

"Everyone welcome. Everyone at home. That's the kind of tree I like," said the Lamb King.

"So what do we do with the little guy in the nut?" asked the Lemur.

"We leave him here," suggested the Lamb King, attaching the nut—they couldn't see how—to a low-hanging branch. "We take him from the Me Tree and put him in—what should we call it?—the We Tree! And, maybe, on this tree he will start to grow again and find his way out."

"So," said Lily, looking up at the We Tree, "can I climb it?"

"High as you like," grinned the Lamb King.

"And I'd rather like to meet that squirrel," said the Lemur, clambering up the trunk.

"Why not?" the Lamb King smiled. "There's room in this tree for everyone!"

4. THE ICE-CREAM VAN

"Do you hear that?" asked the Lemur. "That music, off in the distance?"

"I do!" said Lily. "It's an ice-cream van. It's got to be!"

"Well, we're in a playground, after all," the Lamb King grinned. "And it's summertime. So there has to be an ice-cream van. What's your favourite flavour?"

"Chocolate with caramel sauce," said Lily dreamily.

"Mango and coconut, covered in tiny little grubs," said the Lemur.

"Ugh!" said the Lamb King. "To each their own, I guess. Me, I like strawberry."

"So, what are we waiting for?" demanded the Lemur. "There's no point just talking about ice cream. Let's go get some!"

Then off they raced—Lily, the Lemur and the Lamb King.

But as the music from the ice-cream van grew louder, the path they were running on grew narrower and narrower. And narrower still. Until,

THE ICE-CREAM VAN

at last, they came to a bridge. A bridge that bridged a little stream. A bridge that was so thin, it could only be crossed one at a time.

And there, stepping onto the bridge just before them, was…

"A Slow Loris!" cried the Lemur. "We'll never get there if we have to walk behind a Slow Loris!"

"Maybe he's not so slow," said Lily. "Maybe he's a Fast Loris."

"There is no such thing as a Fast Loris!" the Lemur sighed. "The clue is in the name."

"Your friend is right," said the Loris. Slowly. "We are slow. Very slow. Exceedingly slow. Slower than most slow things."

"Slower than snails?" asked Lily.

The Loris thought about her question. Slowly.

"Not quite," he replied, at last. "But we are working on it."

"Maybe you could work on getting out of the way," suggested the Lemur.

"I don't think I can," said the Loris. "This bridge is very narrow."

"I could hop over you," said the Lemur. "It would take maybe just one little bounce off your back. I'm very light."

"But *I* couldn't do that," said Lily.

"Me neither," said the Lamb King. "Maybe we should just wait."

"Wait?!" cried the Lemur. "Look! There are already loads of people in front of the ice-cream van. By the time we get there, all the best grubs will be gone."

"That is a pity," said the Loris. "I'm fond of grubs,

myself. In fact, I used to have a friend who was a grub. I could tell you the story, if you like."

"Will it take long?" the Lemur sighed.

"Of course," said the Loris. "Slowly is the only way we know how to tell stories."

"I want to hear it!" said Lily.

"Me, too," agreed the Lamb King.

"If you must," said the Lemur. "I guess there's nothing else to do as we walk, ever so slowly, across this bridge."

"It was many years ago…" the Loris began.

"And many years until we get our ice cream," muttered the Lemur.

"I was just minding my own business," continued the Loris, "walking slowly through the jungle, appreciating the trees and the flowers and the other animals, when I heard a cry for help."

"Was it the grub?" asked Lily.

"It was," the Loris replied. "It took me a long time to find him, though."

"No surprise there," whispered the Lemur.

"Shush!" said Lily.

"I looked here. And there. And here again. And there again. And here once more. Always following his little grub voice. Until finally I found him, trapped in a spider's web."

"Oh dear!" cried Lily.

"He looked so pitiful," the Loris went on. "His

little grub hands were shaking. There were tears in his little grub eyes. He knew exactly what would happen, once that spider returned to its web. It's the way of things, I suppose. Weaker things are preyed upon by stronger things."

"But it doesn't have to be that way, does it?" suggested the Lamb King.

"My thoughts exactly," said the Loris. "And that is why I freed him..."

"And gobbled him up?" chuckled the Lemur.

"*Lemur!*" cried Lily.

"... and sent him on his way," the Loris concluded. "We have, of course, been friends ever since that day. And I have watched, with more than a little pride, at what he has accomplished."

"Well, what *we* have accomplished—finally—is crossing this bridge!" exclaimed the Lemur. Then he sighed. They were standing at the very back of the most enormous queue.

"We're last," groaned the Lemur.

But that was when a voice rang out from the ice-cream van.

"Boris! Boris the Loris! Is that you, my friend?"

"It is!" replied the Loris. Slowly.

"Make way, everyone," the voice shouted. "Make way for my friend!"

"Can my new friends come too?" Boris called back.

"Of course!" came the reply.

So Boris the Loris and Lily, the Lemur and the Lamb King made their way—ever so slowly—to the front of the queue.

Where they stood, at last, before the ice-cream van.

Grubby's Ice-Cream Van. That was what the sign said.

And in the van there was an army of grubs, lifting up cones and scooping up ice cream, with Grubby leading the way.

"We thought we'd be last. But now we're first!"

THE ICE-CREAM VAN

Lily laughed. "What a surprise!"

"You knew this would happen all along, didn't you?" said the Lemur to the Loris.

"There's no need to rush to be first, when you have friends," Boris smiled. "So, my friend's gift to me is my gift to you!"

"Now then," interrupted Grubby, inside the ice-cream van. "What are we having today?"

"Strawberry," said the Lamb King.

"Chocolate with caramel sauce," said Lily.

Then they all looked at the Lemur.

"Mango and coconut," he said, "covered in…"

He paused. And looked at his friends. And looked at the grubs.

"Chocolate sprinkles, please!"

5. UPSIDE DOWN

Lily, the Lemur and the Lamb King were in the playground, on the swings.

"I love the swings!" shouted Lily as she swooped up in the air.

"Me too!" said the Lamb King.

"Going back and forth *too* much makes me feel just a little sick," said the Lemur. "But on a hot day like this, any bit of breeze is welcome."

"I wish I could swing so high that I would go round the bar on top," said Lily.

"I tried that once," said the Lamb King. "It's not as fun as it sounds."

"Fun?" cried the Lemur. "It sounds horrible to me! I'm happy to swing ever-so-gently and enjoy the breeze and the view."

"Look, there's a mum and dad," observed Lily. "Taking their little boy out of his pushchair."

"There's a pirate and his pirate friends," said the Lamb King. "And a whole bunch of cabbage people."

"I know I have said it

before, but this is a very strange playground," said the Lemur. "For example, there's a Very Big Bunny over there, about to step on a Very Small Elephant."

"Oh no!" cried Lily and the Lamb King together. And off they rushed to rescue the tiny elephant.

The Lamb King latched onto the Very Big Bunny's leg, as Lily bravely rolled under its foot and grabbed the Very Small Elephant.

"I'm so sorry!" whispered the gigantic bunny, who had a voice like a tiny child. "I did not see that little creature."

And the elephant trumpeted, "Thank you very much!" She had a voice ten times her size. "My name is Bella. Bella the Elephant."

"And I'm just called Bigg," whispered the Very Big Bunny.

"Pleased to meet you," said Lily. "I'm called Lily. And these are my friends, the Lemur and the Lamb King. Would you like to join us on the swings?"

"I don't much like the swings," Bigg whispered.

"And I much prefer the climbing frame," trumpeted Bella.

"Well, let's do that, then!" said the Lamb King.

So up the climbing frame they all went. Lily, the Lemur and the Lamb King. And the rabbit and the elephant too.

"Does this thing have a weight restriction?" asked the Lemur, glancing at Bigg the Bunny.

"Not as far as I know," replied the Lamb King. "I think it's strong enough for everybody."

UPSIDE DOWN

"I have an idea!" Lily shouted. "Let's go to the very top and hang upside down!"

"That is likely to make me feel sick again," complained the Lemur. But up he went anyway.

When everyone was hanging, at last, from the top bar, they all looked around.

"My trunk is hanging down the wrong way," trumpeted Bella. "Or maybe it's hanging up?"

"My ears are hanging down too!" Bigg whispered.

"And my hair," said Lily.

"And yet, strangely, your crown is still on your

head," said the Lemur to the Lamb King.

"It's a very good crown," the Lamb King shrugged, his shoulders moving down and up instead of the other way round!

"Look at the playground, though," he said.

"Everything is upside down there, too!" Lily cried. "At least that's how it looks. The ground is the sky and the sky is the ground!"

"The branches of the trees are on the bottom and the trunks are on the top," said Bigg.

"That would make picking apples easier," said the Lemur. "And pears. And bananas. And... donuts? I never noticed that tree before."

"Everybody can reach them!" said Lily. "Not just people who are tall."

"Or people who can afford ladders!" added the Lamb King.

"And look!" cried Bella the elephant. "All the little animals like me, who run around on the ground, are high above those nasty hawks and eagles who love to swoop down and grab us!"

"So they are," said the Lamb King. "How about that? I guess when you look at the world upside down, everything looks different."

"It's a shame it can't be that way for real," Lily sighed.

"Why not?" asked the Lamb King. "Why shouldn't the weak be the ones on top? Why shouldn't there be food for those who have trouble reaching it? Why shouldn't the world be upside down?"

"Because it would give me a headache!" said the Lemur. "Being upside down all the time. I think I prefer things just the way they are. Right side up."

"I've heard that before," the Lamb King mused. "But we've had a glance, haven't we? So maybe it's time to get down."

"Just one more look," whispered Bigg.

"One long look," agreed Bella.

"So we can remember," said Lily. "What everything looks like, upside down."

Then Lily, the Lemur and the Lamb King made their way down from the climbing frame.

And the rabbit and the elephant too.

"Look! A roundabout!" trumpeted Bella, trundling off in that direction.

"Race you there!" Lily replied.

"I think I'd better be the one who pushes!" suggested Bigg.

"And *I* think I'm going to feel just a little sick," the Lemur sighed. "*Again*."

6. THE APPLE ARGUMENT

Lily, the Lemur and the Lamb King were wandering through the playground. It was a late summer's day. The trees were filled with fruit, ripe for the harvest.

"Look!" said Lily. "Bella and Bigg are up ahead, picking apples. Let's go see them!"

She hoped to have a happy reunion with her new friends. But Bella and Bigg were far from happy.

In fact, they were arguing with each other.

"What's wrong?" asked the Lamb King.

"Everything!" trumpeted Bella. "Where do I start? He stepped on my trunk! He dropped apples

on my head! And I'm pretty sure he's keeping the best ones for himself!"

"That is not fair!" Bigg whispered angrily in his tiny little voice. "I can't help it that my feet are huge and I can't always see where I'm stepping. I only dropped one apple. And I am not keeping the best ones. I'm *not*!"

"Maybe we should take a little walk together,"

THE APPLE ARGUMENT

suggested the Lamb King.

"Not with that bumbling bunny!" grunted Bella.

"Not with that grumpy trunk!" muttered Bigg.

"Do it for my sake," said the Lamb King. "Please?"

"All right," Bella sighed. "But who is going to watch the apples in our baskets?"

"Happy to help!" grinned the Lemur, smacking his lips.

"Lemur!" Lily warned. "She said 'watch', not 'eat'!"

"But surely a little *payment* should be in order," the Lemur said.

"One apple," Bella agreed reluctantly. "Just one!"

"All right," the Lemur smiled, searching at once for the biggest, reddest, ripest one.

"So, where shall we go on our little walk?" asked Bigg.

"There's a lovely field over there," said the Lamb King, pointing. And off they went: Lily, the Lamb King, Bigg and Bella, leaving the Lemur behind.

They walked, but they did not talk. Bigg and Bella were still very angry with one another. So Lily tried her best to start a conversation.

"It's a beautiful day," she began. "Not too hot. A bit of a breeze. Just right. And this field is really very…"

She had meant to say "lovely". But when Lily

looked around, she realized that the field was not lovely. Not lovely at all.

"Where did all these nettles come from?" she cried. "And these thorn bushes and weeds? They weren't here a minute ago."

And the further they walked, the higher the nettles and weeds and thorn bushes grew!

"I don't think this was a very good idea," said Bigg. "It's not a very nice place."

"And I can't see a thing down here!" Bella trumpeted. Then she shouted "Ouch!" and "Ouch!" again.

"What's the matter?" asked Bigg.

"I stepped on a thorn! It's stuck in my foot," Bella cried.

"Oh, no!" said Bigg. Then he reached down, picked up the little elephant, and gave her a good looking-over—turning her one way, and then another.

"Stop shaking me about!" Bella trumpeted. "I

don't like being shaken."

"I'm just searching for the thorn," Bigg explained. "There it is!"

Bigg tried removing the thorn, but his paws were… well… too big. So he looked down at Lily and the Lamb King and asked for their help.

"No problem," said the Lamb King. And as Bigg held Bella above him, he gently pulled out the thorn.

THE APPLE ARGUMENT

"Thank you," Bella said to the Lamb King. "And I suppose you deserve a thank you, too," she said to Bigg. "In spite of all the shaking."

And then she smiled. "Perhaps I was a bit too harsh. Before, I mean."

"And maybe I should have been more careful," Bigg admitted. "So, how about I carry you back—carefully—so you don't step on another thorn?"

"I don't think that will be a problem," said Lily. "Look!"

Wave after wave of the nettles and thorns and weeds around them began to shrink. And when they had all died away, in their place a bright red field of poppies appeared.

"How did that happen?" Lily wondered.

The Lamb King shrugged. "It's obviously a very sensitive piece of land!"

Then through the poppies they waded, and

returned at last to the apple tree.

The Lemur was sitting beneath it, his belly bulging, and the baskets half-full.

"Lemur!" Lily shouted. "What have you done? We told you that you could only have one!"

"Well, I had one," he burped. "And then another one. And another one after that. Surely you understand. Because we're all friends, right?"

Bigg looked at Bella. Bella looked at Bigg. They both looked at the Lemur.

"Right!" they agreed.

"Let's get picking, then!" the Lemur grinned. "As soon as I get up, of course..."

And he gave a very loud, very satisfied burp.

7. NAN'S HANDBAG

Lily's Nan stared at the Scrabble board.

Her handbag sat on the ground beside her, amid the first fall of early autumn leaves. And the cupcakes she had made were in a box at the end of the table.

"Yes!" Nan shouted at last, placing the letters on the board. "Triple word score!"

"Here we go again," moaned the Lemur.

"Nan always wins," said Lily.

"My turn," said Boris the Loris. And everyone sighed.

"Your new friend takes a very long time to take his turn," Nan whispered.

"He's a Slow Loris," Lily explained.

"Or quite possibly a Very Slow Loris," added the Lemur.

"A Very Slow Loris," Boris smiled. "One day, perhaps. I can only dream."

"Well, at least I've got plenty of time to eat this cupcake," said the Lemur, wiping the previous cupcake's icing from his lips.

"You'll make yourself sick," Lily told him.

"With Nan's cupcakes? Never!" the Lemur replied.

And that was when the Lamb King arrived.

"Nan, this is my other new friend," Lily explained. "He's called the Lamb King."

Nan looked up from her cupcake. She looked hard at the Lamb King. And then she looked puzzled.

"I think we've met before," she said. "Am I right in remembering that?"

"A very long time ago," the Lamb King replied. "But it's been ages since we talked."

Nan looked at Lily. She looked even more puzzled.

"There's no use asking," Lily shrugged. "He won't explain. Or, if he does, you won't understand it. So just play along."

"That's what we do," said the Lemur, reaching for yet another cupcake.

And Boris slowly asked, "Is there a word that both begins and ends with a 'z'?"

"ZZZZZZ!" suggested the Lemur. "Which is the sound we'll all be making if you don't take your turn some time this century!"

"It doesn't matter anyway," said Nan, checking the scores. "He can't possibly catch me."

Boris chuckled. "I can't catch *anything*!"

"And I have a few lady friends I need to be *catching* up with," said Nan. "So, why don't we call it a day?"

"I suppose your lady friends... erm... like cupcakes too?" wondered the Lemur.

"Lemur!" Lily exclaimed.

"As a matter of fact, they are all watching their weight," Nan grinned. "Take the box. It's all yours. It will save me carrying it back to the motorbike."

"Motorbike?" said Boris. "You ride a motorbike?"

"Have done for more years than I can count," answered Nan. "And I'm not giving it up until they drag my wrinkled fingers from the handlebars. Why? Would you like a ride?"

Boris nodded his head. Slowly. But surely. "Yes, please! I would love that!"

The Lamb King laughed out loud. "A Slow Loris on a fast motorbike? Now that would be a true wonder."

"It's my secret pleasure," Boris whispered. "But you must promise to never mention it to any other Loris you might happen to meet. I have a reputation to maintain."

"Cross my heart," the Lamb King promised.

"I parked it just outside the playground gate," said Nan. "You can have a look if you like."

Everyone got up from their chairs.

The Lemur picked up the cupcake box. Lily picked up the Scrabble set. And Nan picked up her handbag. But when she did so, the Lamb King noticed something.

"Do you want some help with that?" he asked. "It looks very heavy."

"Nan keeps everything in there!" Lily explained,

with a smile.

"So she does," agreed the Lamb King.

And Nan just clutched her handbag closer.

Lily and the Lemur ran ahead. The Loris lagged behind. And the Lamb King repeated his offer to Nan.

"I remember now," she answered. "You made that offer once before."

"And you declined," said the Lamb King. "But your handbag looks much heavier now. So, I thought I'd offer again."

"I see," said Nan. "But I've got used to the weight. I can carry it myself."

"That's what everybody thinks," said the Lamb King.

"Until they let me carry it. Go on. You won't believe the difference it will make."

Slowly, Nan loosened her grip. Quietly, she looked inside. Then, carefully, she handed her bag to the Lamb King.

"Does Lily know?" she asked.

"She'll work it out, in the end," he smiled, as he slung the bag over his shoulder.

Then Boris crunched up behind them, through the leaves.

"I can't believe I caught up!" he chuckled. "I never catch up with anyone."

Finally, they all caught up with Lily and the Lemur, who were waiting at the playground gate.

Nan put on her helmet and her goggles and climbed onto her motorbike.

"I don't have time to give you that ride today," she said to Boris. "But one day, I promise."

"Oooh, Nan!" said Lily. "Don't forget your handbag!"

LILY, THE LEMUR AND THE LAMB KING

She took it from the Lamb King and held it out to her nan.

"It's not heavy!" she exclaimed. "Not heavy at all!"

"How about that," said the Lamb King.

"Thank you," said Nan, taking the handbag from Lily. And then, with a rumble and a roar, she was off.

Lily looked at the Lamb King, puzzled. "You look

tired," she said. "I don't think I've ever seen you look tired before."

"Probably just need some sugar," he replied, rubbing his shoulder. "How about sharing one of those cupcakes, Lemur?"

8. TIGERS AND TABLES

Lily, the Lemur and the Lamb King were walking through the park. The leaves on the trees shone red and orange in the late afternoon sun. All was beautiful.

And then something growled.

"Tiger," said the Lamb King.

"Very scary!" cried the Lemur. "Very big!" he added. "And very bitey too!"

"Should we be worried?" asked Lily. "Is it close by?"

"Tigers are everywhere," said the Lamb King. "Whenever anybody gets beaten or bullied or pushed around."

"It happens at school," Lily whispered.

"It happens in the jungle," added the Lemur.

"It happens all over the place," said the Lamb King sadly. "Playgrounds and offices and families and shops. It's the only way some people know how to deal with other people."

"My dad told me how to deal with tigers," said the Lemur. "Give as good as you get. Punch them right back, on their tiger noses."

"And how did that work out for him?" asked the Lamb King.

"Not well," replied the Lemur. "But the tiger did send a kind note to my family, thanking us for the lovely meal."

"Oh, Lemur!" Lily exclaimed.

"It was bound to happen sometime," the Lemur shrugged. "Why my grandparents chose to name him Lunch, I'll never know…"

"There is, of course, another way," said the Lamb King. He walked over to a picnic bench, gently touched the edge, and said, "Not tigers, but… tables!"

And while Lily and the Lemur watched, wide-eyed, the picnic table grew longer and longer and longer still, until the farthest end disappeared down the playground and over the horizon.

"Wow!" said Lily.

"Wow, as well!" agreed the Lemur.

"Just getting started," grinned the Lamb King. Then he touched the table again, and suddenly it was crammed with…

"Cake!" cried the Lemur. "Chocolate cake! And lemon cake! And carrot cake!"

"And cookies!" cried Lily. "Chocolate cookies! And peanut butter cookies! And ginger cookies!"

There were pies, as well. Meat pies and fruit pies too. Apple and pumpkin and cherry. And loaves of freshly baked bread. And vegetables, and dips. A proper harvest feast.

"Is it all for us?" Lily asked the Lamb King.

"Well," he replied, opening his arms wide in welcome, "you... and them!"

And the benches on either side of the table began to fill with people and animals of every description—all talking and laughing and

chattering together.

The Lemur squeezed between a Llama and a little boy, and shoved the biggest piece of cake he could find into his mouth.

"Hang on, just a minute," said the Lamb King. "There's a little something I need the two of you to do."

"What?" the Lemur replied, spraying crumbs everywhere.

"Put these on," said the Lamb King. Then he handed them both an apron. And kept one for himself too.

"Drinks," explained the Lamb King. "Somebody needs to serve drinks to this crowd. And I thought you might like to help me."

"Just as soon as I finish these," said the Lemur, cramming two more pieces of cake into his mouth.

"I would be happy to help!" Lily smiled.

Aprons on and trays at the ready, the three friends made their way along the table. As soon as a drink was ordered, it appeared out of nowhere on the tray, and they handed it to one of the guests.

"It's a very long table," said Lily.

"It looks like it goes on for ever," said the Lemur.

"Exactly," said the Lamb King.

"But how will we get to everybody?" Lily asked.

"With more help," said the Lamb King, pointing down the table. And, sure enough, other people and other animals were putting on aprons and picking up trays too.

"Somebody simply needs to lead the way!" the Lamb King smiled.

So, down the table they went. There was eating and drinking and talking and joking and, after a while, singing and dancing too!

And then something growled.

"Look! It's that tiger!" trembled the Lemur. "What's he doing here?"

"Waiting for a drink, I suppose," guessed the Lamb King.

"So tigers are welcome at the table too?" asked Lily.

"Everyone's welcome," the Lamb King nodded. "Go on. See what he wants."

"I think he wants to eat me," muttered the Lemur. "But if you say so…"

Down to the tiger they went: Lily and the Lemur, one hesitant step at a time.

When they returned, the Lamb King asked, "So…?"

"At first, he did look like he wanted to eat me," said the Lemur. "Like he thought *my* name was Lunch too."

"And he did pound his fist on the table a bit," added Lily, "like he was used to bossing people about."

"But when we asked him if he would like a drink..." said the Lemur.

"... and told him how happy we were to see him," Lily continued, "he smiled..."

"A sharp and toothy smile!" the Lemur trembled. "Then he gave us his order."

"And what did he want?" asked the Lamb King.

"A cup of tea," Lily shrugged.

"Milk. No sugar," added the Lemur.

"What did I tell you?" grinned the Lamb King. "Tigers. And tables!"

9. THE SEESAW

"There's nothing like a lemur," the Lemur insisted. "Even though I say so myself. Big, adorable eyes. Practical prehensile tail. And a cheeky personality."

"Some might say 'annoying'," muttered Bigg the Bunny. "But everyone knows that *bunnies* are cute and bouncy and adorable."

"Not when they're ten feet tall!" trumpeted Bella the Elephant.

"And bounciness isn't everything," added Boris the Loris. Slowly. "There is a lot to be said for animals that take their time going from place to place, savouring the scenery and making the very best of each moment."

"Like the story of the tortoise and the hare," suggested Nan.

"A bit speedy for my liking," said Boris. "Tortoises, I mean. But I take your point."

"Tortoises," Grubby grunted, "are no friends of insects."

But before he could say anything more, Lily and the Lamb King came walking by.

"What are you doing?" Lily asked her friends.

"Nothing much," said the Lemur. "Just trying to figure out which animal is best."

"Which animal is best?" chuckled the Lamb

THE SEESAW

King. "I have the perfect answer to that question. Follow me!"

So off they went, across the playground. Lily, the Lemur and the Lamb King. And all of their friends.

"Here it is!" said the Lamb King. "The answer to your question!"

"It's a seesaw," grunted the Lemur. "How is a seesaw going to tell us which of us is the best?"

"Very simply!" the Lamb King replied. "One of you sits on each side, and the one on the side that goes down will be the best."

"Surely the enormous rabbit will win every time, then," said Boris. "He's heavier than all of us."

"All of us put together!" added Grubby.

"Trust me. It's not about weight," said the Lamb King. "To prove that, let's start with someone other than Bigg, shall we? How about Boris and the Lemur?"

So Boris the Loris climbed on one end. Slowly. And the Lemur popped onto the other end. Everyone watched, as the seesaw teetered up and down, then stopped with both sides...

"Equal!" shouted Lily. "You're both best!"

"Or maybe we just weigh the same," the Lemur sighed.

"Then perhaps we should put the bunny on one end," suggested the Lamb King. "And the grub on the other."

So Boris and the Lemur got off the seesaw, and Grubby and Bigg got on.

And by the time the seesaw stopped teetering, the result was...

"Equal again!" Bella trumpeted. "So it can't be the weight!"

"Hop off!" ordered Nan. "I'll have a look underneath. Maybe there's something wrong with the mechanism."

"Nan's very good at fixing things," whispered Lily to the Lamb King. "She does all the work on her motorbike. If there's anything wrong, she'll find it."

Nan poked around under the seesaw, jiggling one thing and prodding another. When she emerged, she announced, "It all looks fine to me. Even though it defies the laws of gravity."

The Lamb King grinned. "Maybe there are other laws. Let's see what happens when you and Lily hop on."

So Nan sat down on one end and Lily climbed onto the other. And the result was...

"The same, again," said Lily. Then she noticed something. "Bella hasn't been on the seesaw," she said.

"Yes, well, I'm not a big fan of seesaws," Bella explained. "Too uppy and downy for my liking. But if you insist, I'll have a go."

"Not that there are likely to be any surprises," muttered the Lemur.

So the little elephant trundled onto the low end of the seesaw, and Bigg the Bunny hopped onto the other end.

Everyone expected the two ends to level up, just as they had before. But this time, the end that Bella stood on refused to rise. And, hop hard as he might, Bigg could not persuade his end to go down!

"Now what?" complained the Lemur. "It doesn't make sense!"

"It's all very curious," replied the Lamb King. "But I have an idea."

Then he leaned over Bella, and paused, like he was listening. Listening very closely.

"A heartbeat!" he whispered. "Just as I thought."

And then he announced: "Bella, you have a tiny little elephant growing inside of you! And that means there are two of you at this end of the seesaw. You and your little baby. And two is more than one! Even one great big bunny at the other end."

Bella trumpeted with joy and slid carefully off her end of the seesaw. Bigg's end fell down with a crash. But he didn't mind. He was just happy for Bella.

And so was everyone else.

They hopped and jumped and cheered—and, in Boris' case, moved about very slowly—to celebrate the new life, growing for all it was worth, inside their little elephant friend.

When the cheering was done, Lily said, "Why don't we try some different combinations?"

So that was what they did:

Boris and Grubby.

Bigg and Lily.

Nan and Lemur.

But each and every time, the seesaw declared that the individual on one end was as good as the one on the other.

"Looks like everyone is worth exactly the same!" the Lamb King concluded.

"So nobody's best?" Lily asked.

"Or maybe everybody is," the Lamb King grinned. "That's what the seesaw says."

"But, surely, a prehensile tail and big, adorable eyes..." said the Lemur.

"Are just different," said the Lamb King. "And maybe *different* really is what's best, after all!"

10. THE HERMIT

Lily, the Lemur and the Lamb King were on their way to the playground. The winter air had just started to bite, but the day was sunny. The perfect time for a walk.

They turned a corner, and suddenly the walking stopped. Something was blocking their way.

"That wasn't here yesterday," said the Lamb King.

"No, it wasn't," grumbled the Lemur. "But I'm not surprised. There's always something blocking the roads, isn't there? Potholes. Construction. Cones. Anything to get in the way of normal ordinary lemurs going about their business!"

When the Lemur had finished his rant, Lily

simply asked, "What is it?"

"It's big," observed the Lamb King.

"Massive!" agreed the Lemur.

"It's sort of a kind of house," said Lily. "Isn't it?"

"Strangest house I've ever seen," the Lemur grunted.

"It looks a bit like a seashell," said Lily.

The Lamb King walked up and touched it.

"Doesn't feel like a seashell," he said. "Some of it's wood. Some of it's plastic. There's no shell in it at all."

THE HERMIT

"Put your ear to it," Lily chuckled. "Maybe you'll hear the sea."

So the Lamb King did. And that was when a little door opened at the base of the seashell house and a little someone stormed out. Someone quite crabby. Someone who was, in fact, a crab.

"And what exactly do you think you're doing?" the crab crabbed.

"Nothing," said the Lamb King, stepping back. "Just trying to figure out what this is."

"It's my house!" the crab shouted. "And I'll thank you to leave it alone."

"Why wasn't it here yesterday?" asked the Lemur.

"I would have thought that was obvious!" the crab shouted again. "I am a hermit crab. And we are always on the move, in search of bigger and better houses."

"But you're not very big," said Lily. "And your house is huge! We learned in school that hermit crabs only move when they outgrow their shells. So why would you need a bigger one?"

The crab sighed. A long, frustrated sigh. "Because I am a very special hermit crab," he replied.

"Special, how?" asked the Lamb King, intrigued.

"This is not something I would freely share with just anyone," said the crab. "But you look more trustworthy than most. So I shall tell you what makes me special."

Then he waved a claw to draw the Lamb King and his friends closer.

He paused. He smiled. And then he whispered, "Shiny things."

"What shiny things?" asked the Lemur.

"The shiny things in my house," the crab grinned. "It's full of them. Full to bursting. And that is why I need a bigger house."

"What kind of shiny things?" asked Lily.

THE HERMIT

"The very best kind," replied the crab. "The kind that can only be found by the sea. There is a window at the very top. Have a look if you like."

The Lemur leaped onto the Lamb King's shoulders and then onto his head. From there he hopped on top of the house and looked into the window. Then he climbed back down, with a puzzled look on his face.

"Did you see them?" asked Lily. "Did you see the shiny things?"

"I did," the Lemur nodded.

"So, what are they?" said the Lamb King. "Coins? Jewels?"

"Erm, no," said the Lemur. "You know those little things you pull when you want to open a can of soda? The house is full of *them*."

"Pop tabs!" exclaimed the Lamb King. "But they're worth..."

"Everything!" the crab cried. "They're shiny and silvery and simply divine! I have spent my whole life collecting them. Filling one house and then another, and another. House after house after house. Those other hermit crabs were content with shells that could only contain themselves. But once I discovered these shiny things, I simply had to have more. And more shiny things demanded more room."

"But they're just pop tabs," said the Lemur.

"Just pop tabs?" the crab sneered. "I've lost track of the times I've heard that. Crabs can be so cruel. And it's clear that you are as blind as they are. My lovely precious shiny things mean everything to me, so I have left the life of the average hermit crab behind, and set out on my own, travelling from one body of water to another, in search of that which makes my life special!"

"But what about your family?" asked Lily. "Don't you miss them?"

"Not when they get in the way of making my dream come true," said the crab.

"And when *will* your dream come true?" the Lamb King asked.

"When I have all the shiny things I need," the crab replied. "And a house big enough to hold them. Then, and only then, will I sit back and say to myself, 'Well done. Relax. Be happy. For now you have all that you will ever need!'"

"I see," said the Lamb King. "Well, we were on our way to our playground. Perhaps you would like to join us."

"Are there shiny things there?" asked the crab.

"In the bins," the Lemur muttered, so that only Lily could hear.

"I'm not sure," said the Lamb King. "But there are plenty of other valuable things you might learn to love."

"Don't think so," the crab grunted. "Only shiny things will do. Goodbye to you, then."

But as he waved his claw, something dropped down from the sky. Something from the sea, as it happened. But not something shiny. Something big. Something hungry.

And before the Lamb King and his friends could react, a huge seagull scooped up the crab in its beak and flew away!

Lily, the Lemur and the Lamb King looked at one another, shocked.

"I did not expect that," said the Lemur, at last.

"I don't think he did, either," said the Lamb King.

"Poor little crab," whispered Lily, wiping away a tear. "He spent his whole life collecting those shiny things, and now he's gone. That's so sad."

"Yes, it is," the Lamb King nodded. "In so many ways."

"So, what do we do now?" asked Lily. "With his house, I mean."

"Well, I don't want a giant fake shell full of pop tabs," the Lemur grunted, "do you?"

"Can't say that I do," replied the Lamb King. "Why don't we push it out of the way, so that it no longer blocks the path?"

So that was what they did. Lily, the Lemur and the Lamb King.

Then off to the playground they went, in the winter air, wondering about crabs and gulls and shiny things.

11. NOT THAT KIND OF KING

Lily, the Lemur and the Lamb King were walking in the first deep winter's snow. And all their friends were walking with them. Apart from Nan, who wasn't feeling very well.

Bella the elephant was perched on Bigg the Bunny's shoulder. And Grubby rode on the back of Boris the Loris. Slowly—of course!—as they made their way through the snow.

"I have a question," said the Lemur to the Lamb King. "It's been bugging me for quite some time now. You're a king, right? You have the crown and all. But we never see you do any king things."

LILY, THE LEMUR AND THE LAMB KING

"What do you mean?" asked the Lamb King.

"Well, if I was king," the Lemur replied, "say, king of the lemurs, I'd do quite a lot of ordering people about. *Fetch me a mango!* I would say to my lemur lackeys. And then, *Fetch me another one!*"

"I see," the Lamb King nodded. "Well, I'm not that kind of king."

"The kind of king who doesn't like mangoes?" replied the Lemur. "Who doesn't like mangoes?"

The Lamb King lifted a hoof to explain, but Boris got there first.

"If I was king," he said, slowly and deliberately, "I would put a speed limit on everything! No one would be allowed to move any faster than—let us say, just for argument's sake—the fastest Loris."

"Which means that no one would get anywhere!" sighed the Lemur.

"On the other hand, they would all have time to enjoy the scenery," Boris replied.

"I see what you mean," said the Lamb King. "And in some ways it could be a good thing. But I'm not that kind of king."

Then Grubby spoke up.

"If I was king," he began, looking at the Lemur, "I would take revenge on every grub-munching monster, so there would no longer be any threats to us peace-loving grubs, who simply want to go about our business in safety."

"I'm definitely not that kind of king," the Lamb King said.

"What about a beautiful palace?" trumpeted Bella. "If I was queen, that's what I would have. A palace dressed in jewels and silk and every other fancy thing. With a massive throne in the middle."

"But how would you get up on the throne?" asked Bigg.

"With a purpose-made throne-lift!" Bella proudly trumpeted.

"Sounds lovely," the Lamb King grinned. "And clever, to boot. But I'm not that kind of king."

NOT THAT KIND OF KING

"Then what kind of king are you?" asked Lily.

The Lamb King stopped. It looked like he was thinking. But what he was actually doing was listening.

"Do you hear that?" he asked.

And everyone shook their heads.

"Someone's in trouble," he said. "Maybe more than one someone. Follow me."

Then off they went, through the snow. And they came, at last, to a fallen tree. Branches were everywhere. And in the middle of two branches, crossed over one another like an X, they found a family of squirrels, huddling together in the cold.

"What happened?" asked the Lamb King.

"The wind blew our tree down," explained the littlest squirrel. "The tree is where our home was. We're hurt and we're cold. Can you help us, please?"

"Of course we can," said the Lamb King. Then he sat down in the snow next to the squirrels.

"You'll get all wet!" worried Lily.

But the Lamb King took no notice. Instead, he reached out a hoof and tore a piece of fleece from his woolly coat. He wrapped it around the littlest squirrel. Then he did it again and again and again, till every squirrel was wrapped up warm and tight.

The squirrels were saved, but there was almost no wool left on the Lamb King at all. He was shivering and trembling.

"You'll catch your death of cold!" cried Bella.

"What can we do?" asked the Lemur.

"What's going on?" asked Boris, who had only just arrived.

"I have an idea!" cried Lily. "Everyone gather round!"

And that was what they did. They crowded round their friend, hoping that their fur and their coats would keep him warm.

"This is all very good," said the Lemur, after a while. "But we can't stay here for ever."

"I don't think you'll need to," the Lamb King replied, no longer shivering. "Look!"

The friends let go of one another, and when they looked down, the Lamb King was covered in wool once again!

"How did that happen?" asked Grubby.

"It's a mystery," shrugged the Lamb King. "I helped the squirrels. You helped me. Maybe that's just how things work in the playground."

"Speaking of the squirrels," said Lily. "They're not cold anymore, but they're still hurt and they're still here. Shouldn't we take them to another tree and help find them a new home?"

"Yes, please!" squeaked all the squirrels together.

"An excellent idea," the Lamb King agreed, holding out his hoof for the littlest squirrel to climb onto.

Everyone else did the same, and they made their way through the snow towards a new tree, one that looked big and strong.

But as they went, the Lemur looked at Lily and whispered, "He never answered the question, did he? I mean about the king thing? If he's not the kind of king who gives orders, what kind of king is he?"

Lily looked at the squirrels in their warm woollen coats and smiled. "Oh, I'm pretty sure he did answer you," she replied. "I think he's the kind of king who gives himself away."

12. FOR EVER

Lily sat on her bench in the playground. The Lemur perched quietly at her side. It was spring again, but neither of them were feeling springy.

Then the Lamb King sat down and joined them. "I heard about your nan," he said softly.

Lily wiped one eye with the back of her hand. "I really miss her," she whispered.

"I know," he whispered back. There was nothing more to say. So, for a while, they all just sat there, quietly.

"She made great cakes," Lily said, at last.

"I loved her cakes," nodded the Lamb King.

"Me, too," added the Lemur. "Particularly the ones with the little sugar flowers on top."

"And she was brilliant at games," Lily went on.

"A Scrabbling genius," the Lamb King agreed. "And what about her woodwork? And her plumbing? She could fix anything."

"Even that old motorbike of hers," the Lemur sighed. "I loved riding on the handlebars!"

Lily smiled weakly. "Handy Nan. That's what everybody called her."

Then everything grew dark. Just a bit dark at

first. And then darker, and darker still.

"Are you doing that?" Lily asked the Lamb King.

"I think that's you," he replied. "Sadness, and grief, and having to say goodbye will do that."

"It's scary," said Lily, as the dark grew even darker. "When will it stop?"

"It takes time," said the Lamb King. "But this might help. Follow me."

"Follow you?" the Lemur replied. "We can hardly see you!"

"Follow the sound of my voice, then," he said. "I'll keep talking. You keep listening. I'll be there. I promise."

So they set off into the dark. The Lamb King up front, and Lily and the Lemur right behind.

"Careful," said the Lamb King. "Here's a little step. Take your time. Ooh, looks like we're heading downhill now. And it's a little slippery."

As he talked, Lily and the Lemur listened. To his voice, but also to the sound of their footsteps. Leaves shuffled beneath them at first. And then the grinding of gravel. After that came the silence of dust. Then, finally, the hard echo of Lily's shoes on stone.

"We're there," said the Lamb King.

"Where?" asked Lily.

"At the end of our journey," the Lamb King answered, mysteriously. "And at the beginning of one, as well. You'll see."

And, just like that, Lily and the Lemur did. Right in front of them, something like a door opened.

FOR EVER

It didn't swing open or lift open—it rolled open. And they had to hide their eyes from the light that poured in and chased every shadow away.

When at last they could look around, they were greeted by rock. Rock walls, a rock ceiling and a rock floor.

"Looks like a cave," said the Lemur.

"Something like that," the Lamb King replied. Then he pointed out through the open door.

"Do you see those women?" he asked.

Lily nodded.

"They feel a lot like you do. Their friend died just three days ago, and they miss him so much, it hurts. They are on their way here to put spices on his body."

"To this cave?" asked Lily, puzzled.

"To this tomb," said the Lamb King solemnly. "The end of one journey."

Then he smiled a reassuring smile. "But the women are in for a surprise, because their friend has already begun a new journey and they will not find him here. He's alive again, you see. Risen from the dead!"

"Did you know their friend?" asked Lily.

But before the Lamb King could reply, suddenly, from somewhere deep in the cave behind them, came the sound of voices. Murmuring, at first. And then louder, and louder still. A huge crowd.

And the Lamb King smiled again and said, "It's time to go. Me first. That's how it works. And then the rest of you, following behind. All of us, out of the tomb."

So the Lamb King stepped out into the light. And Lily and the Lemur followed. Then, as the Lamb King walked over to the women, that great crowd poured out from the tomb behind them. Their murmuring had turned to laughter and cheering and shouts of joy.

But there was only one sound that mattered to Lily.

The roar of a motorbike engine! She knew it the moment she heard it. And she knew her nan, as well, even though she looked very different from the woman Lily had said goodbye to only a few days before. She seemed old and young at the same time, somehow. Was that possible?

Handy Nan popped off her saddle, and while the Lemur hopped onto the handlebars, Lily shut her eyes and hugged her nan for what seemed like for ever.

LILY, THE LEMUR AND THE LAMB KING

But when she opened her eyes again, Nan had gone, and Lily and the Lemur and the Lamb King were back on the bench in the playground.

"I wanted to stay!" cried Lily. "Why couldn't I stay?"

"It wasn't your time," whispered the Lamb King. "You have this journey to finish. And grandchildren of your own to impress with your motorbiking skills, one day. Until then, hold onto that hug. One day, it will last for ever in a place where we will all be together. I promise."

"But where? And when? And how?" Lily sighed.

"In this playground," smiled the Lamb King. "Or something very much like it. Only better. And bigger. Big as the whole world!"

"What do we do in the meantime?" asked the Lemur.

"We play!" said the Lamb King. "And we welcome everybody we know to play along with us. Like Boris, and Grubby, and Bella and Bigg. Oh, and that tiger too!"

Then he pointed. "Look, here they come!"

And when they were all gathered, off they went. Lily, the Lemur, the Lamb King, and all of their friends. Walking through the playground. On the path to for ever.

The stories you've just read were all inspired by a real person: Jesus.

A little like the Lamb King, Jesus invites us into a kingdom where not everything is quite as you might expect.

To find out more, read on...

1. THE LAMB KING

This story is inspired by what happened at the beginning of the world. The Bible says,

> *In the beginning God created the heavens and the earth. (Genesis 1:1)*

What is creating? It's playing, simple as that. Just look at some of the incredible, amusing, outrageous, beautiful creatures God made when he made the world. Pangolins and platypuses. Hummingbirds and hammerhead sharks. I'm pretty sure you could name lots more. You couldn't make them up, if you tried. But God did!

And he wants us to use our imaginations too. God gives us the gift of his breath—his Spirit—living inside us. That means we can fill the world he gave us with even more outrageous, playful beauty!

2. TOMORROW AND TODAY

This story is inspired by something Jesus said.

> *Do not worry, saying, "What shall we eat?" or "What shall we drink?" or "What shall we wear?" For the pagans run after all these things, and your heavenly Father knows that you need them. (Matthew 6:31-32)*

I wonder what kind of things you find yourself worrying about. Food? Clothes? Faraway hawks? Fortunately, Jesus says we don't have to worry. God knows what we need. So instead of thinking about what might happen tomorrow, we can enjoy everything God has given us today.

What a relief!

3. THE ME TREE

This story is inspired by something Jesus said.

> *The kingdom of heaven is like a mustard seed, which a man took and planted in his field. Though it is the smallest of all seeds, yet when it grows, it is the largest of garden plants and becomes a tree, so that the birds come and perch in its branches. (Matthew 13:31-32)*

A mustard seed is hardly any bigger than a dot, but it grows and grows into a gigantic tree. A little like the We Tree, you might say—with room for everyone. Jesus' kingdom is like that too. Sometimes it can seem as small or unimpressive as a tiny seed, but the truth is, it's the greatest kingdom in the world! And who gets to be part of it? Anyone. Everyone.

We're all invited!

4. THE ICE-CREAM VAN

This story is inspired by what Jesus did for everyone who follows him. The Bible tells us,

> *For it is by grace you have been saved, through faith—and this is not from yourselves, it is the gift of God—not by works, so that no one can boast. (Ephesians 2:8-9)*

Grace is what happens when you get something you don't deserve. Boris deserved the favour he received from Grubby, but the rest of the gang didn't. That "first place in the line" was Boris's gift to them.

God gave us a gift just like that too. He sent Jesus to forgive us and to patch up our broken relationship with him, even though we didn't deserve it.

Jesus moved us from "last" to "first"!

5. UPSIDE DOWN

To understand this story, look at what Jesus' mother, Mary, sang about God:

He has scattered those who are proud
  in their inmost thoughts.
He has brought down rulers from their thrones
  but has lifted up the humble.
He has filled the hungry with good things
  but has sent the rich away empty. (Luke 1:51-53)

When Mary sang her song of praise to God, she celebrated a world where everything would be turned upside down. And that's just what Jesus did. In his day and in his time, it was only men with power who mattered. But Jesus welcomed the outcasts, and the poor, and women and children.

And that, quite literally, changed the world!

6. THE APPLE ARGUMENT

This story has something to do with these words that Jesus said:

> *Blessed are the peacemakers, for they will be called children of God. (Matthew 5:9)*

It's easy to fall out with someone—even a friend. What can be hard is putting that friendship back together again. That's why Jesus said that peacemakers are "blessed" and "sons of God", because fixing what has fallen apart requires the kind of patience and understanding and forgiveness that God is so good at giving.

Fortunately, that peacemaking gift is something God gives to each of his followers too—and then we can learn how to pass it on to one another.

7. NAN'S HANDBAG

The Bible says,

> *Surely he took up our pain and bore our suffering. (Isaiah 53:4)*

Hundreds of years before Jesus was born, the prophet Isaiah was given a picture of someone who would come to take away all that was wrong in our lives by carrying it himself. That definitely includes our sins—the things we have done wrong. But Jesus also wants to relieve us of the load of everything else that weighs us down—our sorrow, our grief, our regrets.

I don't know what was in Nan's bag, or what's in yours. I just know we all need someone to carry it for us.

8. TIGERS AND TABLES

This story is inspired by something Jesus did.

> *The Pharisees and the teachers of the law who belonged to their sect complained to his disciples, "Why do you eat and drink with tax collectors and sinners?" Jesus answered them, "It is not the healthy who need a doctor, but those who are ill."*
>
> *(Luke 5:30-31)*

Jesus spent a lot of time at tables. He ate with people who thought they were good. But he also ate with people whom everyone else thought were bad. He was criticized for that, but he always made it clear that tables—and the hospitality that comes with them—were meant for everyone. A place to turn lives around. And a place to turn enemies into friends.

Tigers. And tables!

9. THE SEESAW

This story has something to do with what the Bible says about *us*.

> *For by the grace given me I say to every one of you: do not think of yourself more highly than you ought, but rather think of yourself with sober judgment, in accordance with the faith God has distributed to each of you. (Romans 12:3)*

It's hard to be humble. Because it's easy to think, deep down inside, that we're "better" than that person next to us, or that person over there, or some person on the TV or a social-media site. It makes us feel better about ourselves, I suppose. But God has a better answer for that. He wants us to know that each and every one of us, regardless of our differences, is loved and cherished.

No one's better. Everyone's best!

10. THE HERMIT

This story is inspired by a story Jesus told.

> *The ground of a certain rich man yielded an abundant harvest ...*
>
> *Then he said, "This is what I'll do. I will tear down my barns and build bigger ones, and there I will store my surplus grain. And I'll say to myself, 'You have plenty of grain laid up for many years. Take life easy; eat, drink and be merry.'"*
>
> *But God said to him, "You fool! This very night your life will be demanded from you. Then who will get what you have prepared for yourself?"*
>
> *(Luke 12:16-20)*

Is there something so precious to you that you would give up everything to have it? Fame? Money? Telling other people what to do? Shiny things take many different forms, but just like the crab's pop tabs, they are all worthless compared to loving God and the people around us. And Jesus is pretty clear: if having those shiny things means giving up those more important things, then they are a waste of time. And a waste of a life.

So what's your shiny thing?

11. NOT THAT KIND OF KING

This story is inspired by something Jesus said about himself.

> *For even the Son of Man did not come to be served, but to serve, and to give his life as a ransom for many. (Mark 10:45)*

When Jesus' disciples argued about which of them would rule with him when his kingdom arrived, his answer was simple: being a king is not about being served, it's about serving. And Jesus didn't just talk about that—he actually did it. He served every one of us by giving up his life for us on a cross. And he wants us to follow his example by serving one another.

Jesus is the kind of king who gives himself away!

12. FOR EVER

This story has to do with the Bible's description of the future.

> *Look! God's dwelling place is now among the people, and he will dwell with them. They will be his people, and God himself will be with them and be their God. "He will wipe every tear from their eyes. There will be no more death" or mourning or crying or pain, for the old order of things has passed away. (Revelation 21:3-4)*

God's promise is for a for-ever future, in a new heaven and a new earth. We will be with him, and we will be with each other. We won't be angels with wings, plucking harps and floating on clouds. No, we'll dwell in a new world, remade and renewed! Our bodies will be resurrected, just like Jesus' body was. And we will live, and love, and serve.

And we will play, of course! Why not? The One who brings us joy will be right there, living in the midst of us!